Stories for Young Children and how to tell them

by Mary Medlicott

Illustrated by Martha Hardy

Published 2010 by A&C Black Publishers Limited
36 Soho Square, London W1D 3QY
www.acblack.com

ISBN 9781408124529

First published 2004 as 'Cooking Up A Story' in the UK,
by Featherstone Education
Text © Mary Medicott, 2004
Illustrations © Martha Hardy, 2004
Cover photographs © Shutterstock

Printed in Great Britain by Latimer Trend & Company Limited

This book is produced using paper that is made from wood grown in
managed, sustainable forests. It is natural, renewable and recyclable.

The logging and manufacturing processes conform to the environmental
regulations of the country of origin.

**To see our full range of titles
visit www.acblack.com**

Contents

Welcome to Stories for Young Children and how to tell them!

Storytime is too important to be neglected or treated as just a chore. I believe it can contribute vitally to young children's lives, giving them food for the imagination, nourishment for the emotions and a chance to make sense of the world that we live in. In **Stories for Young Children and how to tell them**, I have brought together some of my best offerings from many years' practical experience of storytime in all kinds of schools and settings throughout the country.

Stories for Young Children and how to tell them originally arose in response to repeated requests from Early Years practitioners in Enfield, one of the most diverse of outer London boroughs. Their requests were for more stories, more rhymes, more hints, more ideas. The resulting book, Cooking Up a Story, now in this new and revised edition with an accompanying CD of its contents, offers a fresh new approach to storytime.

Oral storytelling is an activity that goes back to something very old and precious in human culture. The engagement it creates between storyteller and audience allows plenty of space for imaginative listening and lots of room for participation. Children of all ages love stories told without a book. In the early years, they often respond much better. You'll see them echoing your sounds and gestures, reflecting your facial expressions, taking every opportunity for participating. They join in spontaneously with rhythms, rhymes and repeated phrases. They are eager to say what might happen next and to share the pictures forming in their imaginations. And as you, the storyteller, become aware that they are not only listening but speaking and thinking in an engaged and creative way, it's a wholly magical feeling.

Stories for Young Children and how to tell them offers you a wide selection of stories for telling, as well as a variety of action-chants, rhymes and imagination games.

Many of the items are my own original creations. Some are retellings of traditional tales. All have been tried and tested by me on hundreds of different occasions. I hope the selection provides you with plenty of material for looking again at the unique role that stories and storytime can play in Early Years education.

In each of the nine separate Storytimes into which the book is divided, you will find a highly stimulating rhyme or chant together with a good strong story. Use one or both at any one time or pick and mix as you choose. Each of the sections has its own specially engaging theme such as friendship, surprises or magic but, of course, you can vary the combinations yourself as you extend your repertoire and develop new themes for yourself. Each section also contains hints and advice on how to tell the material in a lively manner and on creative activities to follow.

Some people find it easier to learn stories by hearing rather than reading the story. On the CD that goes with this book (originally published as Talking Up a Story), you can hear me telling all the rhymes, chants and stories that appear in the book together with magical accompanying music specially created and performed by Bill Roberts. Listen to the items while you are making dinner or driving to work. Then try telling one of them yourself at storytime. I know how well they can work both from my own direct experience and from the many hundreds of training sessions I have carried out with Early Years staff and with parents and carers. I hope you will especially enjoy the opening and closing chants that top and tail each session.

As in centuries past, storytelling without the book can give enormous enjoyment to children as well as huge educational benefits. For the adult, it offers a powerful new string to your bow alongside your use of books. I hope you enjoy it every bit as much as the children.

Happy Storytelling!
Mary Medlicott
Storyteller

Introduction

General principles for planning storytime

Allow plenty of time for your storytime. It's not pleasant for storyteller or audience to feel rushed.

Create a well-balanced storytime by mixing and matching rhymes, games and stories.

Keep on telling picture-book stories. Oral storytelling does not mean you have to abandon books.

Repeat your stories on several successive occasions to enable children to get to know them. Familiarity increases children's enjoyment. Plus your stories can be told on demand before and after your storytime sessions.

Bring storytime forward to happen earlier in your morning or afternoon session. The children will be fresher and more attentive and it gives them the opportunity to 'play' with the story afterwards – drawing pictures, helping make props, role-playing the characters or enacting events. You can always have an end-of-session story or rhyme time as well.

Hints on preparing your story for telling

Remembering a story

You may be one of those people who prefers getting to know a story for telling by reading the text. Or you may be someone who prefers to get to know a story by listening to it yourself.

If you choose to read the text, don't try to memorise the story word for word. Instead, read it through a few times, then check if you remember the main points by skimming through it in your mind, noting down the key events or telling it silently to yourself.

If you choose to listen to the stories on the accompanying CD, once familiar with a story set aside time to go through it in your mind, making it suit with your way of thinking and your personal style of talking.

Making the story feel like your own

Spend some time thinking about your chosen story to allow it to sink into your mind. Try closing your eyes and letting yourself dwell on some of the scenes in the story. You will probably find yourself visualizing them in great detail – setting, colours, emotions etc. You can then select the details you want for your telling.

Let the characters in the story talk to each other in your head. Listen to what they say and how they are saying it. This will give you more ideas to add into your telling.

Draw a series of pictures that illustrate your story or make your own story-map of the locations. This will help you to feel that you have located the story in your own mind's eye.

Preparing for participation

There are many ways to attract children's attention and get them joining in with your story. Think through places in the story where you could introduce the following:

- Gestures and actions (a bird flying, a man climbing, an elephant walking)
- Sound effects (an owl hooting, a tap dripping, thunder roaring)
- Dialogue (two people talking, two animals making sounds at each other)
- Rhythms or rhymes (tap your knees for a walking sequence, make up little refrains to repeat in the story)

Children usually need no more encouragement to join in than a friendly smile and an encouraging manner.

Assembling props

It is helpful to find an object or objects – a key, a fish, a comb, a hat – that will make your story visually attractive and help the children to get an idea of what it is about. Getting your props out of a bag helps focus children's attention.

Props do not have to be complicated to be successful. It's often best to have just a few. And you do not have to make use of them during your telling of the story. Showing them first can be equally, or more, effective.

Some people love to use puppets or soft toys. A single soft toy character can provide the basis for a whole series of stories that you make up on the spot. You could have fun by using your newly created stories to reflect recent events at your setting.

Starting and ending your storytime session

Starting your session

A joining-in chant is an excellent way to focus children's attention. You could have a go at making one up. Or, for the one on the CD, start by gently tapping your knees in a rhythmical way. Carry on until you're sure you have gathered the attention of all the children. Then chant these words in time with your tapping:

> It's storytime, it's storytime
>
> Ssh! Listen!
>
> What's going on?

After a pause, repeat the chant, looking round at the children. When you say "Ssh!" put your finger to your lips.

When you say "Listen!" cup your hand around your ear.

Extra interest can be added with some sound-making instruments – a tambourine, a drum, a rainstick, a bell. Set them out in front of you before you start or have them ready in a bag beside you. When everyone is fully engaged, pick up one of the instruments – "Listen!" – and demonstrate its sounds. If you wish, give the children time to talk about the sound before returning to the chant.

Ending your session

There are many traditional endings for stories and storytelling sessions. The one on the CD is as follows. Click your fingers on each word of the first two lines, then for the last line put your hands in front of you and draw them quickly and firmly apart:

> Snip, snap, snout
>
> My story's told out.
>
> And that's the end of it.

Managing your storytime

Where and when storytime takes place has a big effect on the results. Just as it is worth bringing storytime forward in your session at least on some occasions, it is also worth considering the location. Sometimes the book corner is not the best place. There may be more space in another area and it may help you feel freer to tell without a book.

Seating the children in a wide semicircle, in two lines if necessary, allows you to feel near them. It is also worth thinking about sitting in a low chair so that you are not too high above them.

If a child is anxious or unsettled, try moving the child nearer to you. Even better is when there are other adults who can sit with particular children who need help and encouragement to join in. A child who remains unhappy may need to leave the storytime until ready to return. Storytime should be treated as a pleasure which it is a pity to miss.

The length of a storytime session depends on the age and concentration span of the children. Short active sessions with lots of rhymes are best for very young children. Older children should be able to manage longer sessions, but only if they are engaged and enjoying themselves. Younger children can often benefit from being with the older children, especially if the storytime is lively and there's lots of participation. But older children may also need a session of their own with longer and more complex stories.

Disciplining your audience should not be necessary. Rhymes, actions, sounds and gestures should draw the children's attention sufficiently that you don't have to ask them not to fidget.

Special storytime groups

Organising special small storytime groups can be extremely helpful for children who are shy and withdrawn or slow to speak. Small groups give them more adult attention and a better chance to be helped to participate.

A Storytelling Club which happens separately from your regular storytime sessions can help raise the status of storytelling in your group and provide a welcome chance for staff to try out new stories or storytelling ideas.

Mrs Wiggle and Mrs Waggle

– a traditional chant

This popular chant enables children to join in even if they don't have English as a first language or are too young to have developed much language. When the children become familiar with the story, you can vary it by creating new storylines and even changing the characters. This chant is also great for encouraging children to imagine new situations to bring into the story.

Actions

In this action-story, your two thumbs represent Mrs Wiggle and Mrs Waggle and your hands become their houses. Look at the illustrations on the next page to see how to do the actions.

Story summary

One day, Mrs Wiggle goes to see Mrs Waggle, but she's not at home. The next day, Mrs Waggle goes to see Mrs Wiggle but she's not at home. The day after that, the two women both set out to see each other. They meet in the middle!

Full Story
Introducing the characters:

Here's Mrs Wiggle. She's got a house. Look, she's opening the door, she's going inside. Now she's closing the door. Mrs Wiggle has got a friend, Mrs Waggle. Mrs Waggle lives in her own house. Look, she's opening the door and going inside. Now she's closing the door.

Part one of the action:

One morning, Mrs Wiggle woke up early. She decided to go to see her friend. She got ready, opened the door, went out of the house and closed the door. Then she set off.

Up the hill and down the hill, up the hill and down the hill, up the hill and down the hill up and down, until she came to her friend's house.

When she got to Mrs Waggle's, Mrs Wiggle knocked on the door. Knock, knock. No reply.

She knocked again. No reply. She called through the letter-box. "Mrs Waggle... Mrs Waggle..." No reply. So Mrs Wiggle went home, down the hill and up and down, until she got to her house. She opened the door, went inside, closed the door and had a nice cup of tea.

Part two of the action:

The next day, Mrs Waggle woke up in the morning and decided to go and see her friend.

(Repeat the journey that Mrs Wiggle made, including having to go home.)

Part three of the action:

The day after that, Mrs Wiggle and Mrs Waggle both woke up at the same time and both decided to go and see their friend.

(Repeat all the actions as above until the two of them meet on the middle hill.)

"Hello, hello. Fancy seeing you here. I was just coming to see you."
Kiss, kiss, hug, hug.
Then Mrs Wiggle and Mrs Waggle had a nice long chat until it was time for them to go back home. "Bye, Bye. See you later."

So off they went, down the hill and up the hill and down the hill, until they both got home.
Then they each went inside and had a nice cup of tea.

And both of them said the very same thing:
"Isn't it nice to have a friend."

Hints on telling

- Use a little beeping sound to punctuate some of the actions – opening the door, going inside, closing the door. This can amuse the children and help them join in.

- Make extravagant gestures, such as for waking up or drinking a cup of tea. This also helps the story to be amusing.

- Allow the children to remind you of what's about to happen as they pick up the pattern of the story.

- You can elaborate greatly on the story while you tell it. For instance, you could invite your own explanations of why Mrs Wiggle and Mrs Waggle didn't open their door. Maybe they were asleep? Maybe they had already gone out?

- You could extend the storytelling by making up a good gossipy conversation when Mrs Wiggle and Mrs Waggle meet on the hill.

Variations

1. Instead of Mrs Wiggle and Mrs Waggle, your story could be about two men, Mr. Wiggle and Mr. Waggle.

2. When the characters meet on the hill, you could change the story by getting them to play a game, for example, hide-and-seek. As each character goes off to hide, conceal your fist behind your back.

3. Or, after the two characters meet on the hill, divert them to another venue, such as a cafe, a clothes shop, a park or the swimming pool. Use your fingers and thumbs to suggest where they go and what they do.

Mrs Wiggle   opening the door   go inside   closing the door

up hill   down hill   Knock on door   cup of tea

Sun-Frog and Moon-Frog

– retold by Mary Medlicott from a story by
Penny Bernand of Pop-Up Theatre

Sounds and actions make this a thoroughly engaging story for Early Years
children. It affords wonderful opportunities for props and artwork. Its
beautiful ending lifts the story into a different dimension.

❀ Story summary

Two frogs are visited by a strange bird who tells them they are in danger and
offers to help them. They refuse. She returns, they refuse again. The third
time she comes back, they are in real danger and ask for her help. After
taking them to a safe place, she tells them how they can remember her in
future.

🌸 Full Story

Once upon a time, there were two frogs - Moon-Frog and Sun-Frog. They lived in a pond with a rock for jumping and they had a lovely time doing nothing but jumping, staring, blinking, winking and licking the air for flies.

One day they had a visitor – the tikki-tikki bird with her beautiful tail of many-coloured feathers. The tikki-tikki bird said she wanted to help them. Terrible rains were coming; their pond would turn into a rushing river and they would not be safe even though they were used to living in water. She said she could help them find a new pond to move to. But Moon-Frog and Sun-Frog ignored her. "Rubbish!" said Sun-Frog. "Silly!" said Moon-Frog.

Soon the storm began. In the midst of the rain, the tikki-tikki bird returned with her beautiful tail of many-coloured feathers. Once again, Sun-Frog and Moon-Frog didn't want to listen.

After a while, the rain became too heavy even for Sun-Frog and Moon-Frog. At last they found a tree to climb. But by the time they reached the top, there was water all round them. Where were they going to go? What were they going to do? They wished they had listened to the tikki-tikki bird.

Suddenly, the tikki-tikki bird came back. The two frogs asked her to help them. She said she was still willing to take them somewhere safe. This time the two frogs listened. They jumped on her back and she flew through the sky until she came to a place where it was no longer raining. There the frogs saw a different pond where the water was calm. When the tikki-tikki bird flew down, they jumped in the water and started doing what they liked best – jumping, staring, blinking, winking and licking the air for flies.

When the tikki-tikki bird said goodbye, she told them that, in future, when there was sun after rain, if they looked up in the sky, they might see her there and remember that she was their friend. And that is what they did. Every time it finished raining, they looked up in the sky and whenever they saw the rainbow with all its lovely colours, they remembered the tikki-tikki bird and her beautiful tail of many-coloured feathers.

Hints on telling

⊙ Make spectacle eyes when introducing the frogs. Move your elbows up and down to create the sense of two frogs jumping. Make spectacle eyes again to give the sense of the two frogs staring. Use expressive eyes for the winking and blinking. Move your tongue in and out to suggest the two frogs catching flies. When the tikki-tikki bird visits, lift your crossed hands and flap them slowly towards you as she arrives, then away from you when she leaves.

⊙ There's also plenty of opportunity for sound-effects. Children like frog noises – try sinking your voice into your stomach and sucking in your breath as you speak. Just lowering your voice will do. The sounds of the storm can be created by the whole group. For lightning, shoot hands up into the air with a sharp crack of your voice. For thunder, start with hands high up in a fist, then hammering down onto your knees. For rain, start with clicking fingers, then hands brushed together, then fists on knees and finally feet hammering on the floor. The sound of the tikki-tikki bird is as her name suggests: tikki...tikki...

⊙ Props add to the interest of the story. A multi-coloured cloth or a loose plait of multi-coloured ribbons can represent the tikki-tikki bird's tail. Keep it on your lap when you're telling the story and raise it to indicate the tikki-tikki bird's tail each time she arrives on the scene. Then hold it up at the end to represent the rainbow. A soft-toy frog is also a good idea – not to take part in the story but to introduce the characters.

Follow-up activities

Children really enjoy making pictures of this story. Ask them to choose their favourite part of the story and make a picture of that.

Storytime Two

Where's the Sun?
– a traditional English rhyme with actions

Hand movements help young children understand and join in with this magical ryhyme. When they know it, there's plenty of 'imagining' work to be done in visualising the different scenes and making pictures.

What's in there? (make a fist and point into it with the other hand)

Gold and money (look like you're holding and counting money)

Where's my share? (open your hands in an enquiring gesture)

Mousie ran away with it (skitter one hand from side-to-side)

Where's the mousie? (enquiring gesture)

In her housie (make a house shape with your two hands)

Where's her housie? (enquiring gesture)

In the wood (make the usual arm-shape for trees)

Where's the wood? (enquiring gesture)

Fire burned it (flutter your fingers)

Where's the fire? (enquiring gesture)

Water put it out (click fingers to show raindrops)

Where's the water? (enquiring gesture)

Brown bull drank it (lean forward and gulp)

Where's the brown bull? (enquiring gesture)

Back o' Burnie's hill (make a hitch-hiker's thumb to point behind you)

Where's Burnie's hill? (enquiring gesture)

All covered in snow (make a smoothing gesture with both hands)

Where's the snow? (enquiring gesture)

Sun melted it (raise your hands in a circular movement)

Where's the sun? (enquiring gesture)

HIGH, HIGH, UP IN THE SKY (point upwards towards the sky)

Hints on telling

- It is helpful if you change the direction of your gaze between questions and answers – for instance, leftwards for questions, rightwards for answers.

- Make variations in the tone of your voice, not only to emphasise the difference between questions and answers but also to suggest the changing atmosphere, for instance the quiet of the snow-covered landscape.

The Yellow Blob

– an original story by Mary Medlicott

This story emphasises the fun of colour and teaches what happens when you mix yellow and blue.

 ## Story summary

The Yellow Blob lives in a yellow world. One day he comes across a blue lake. After swimming in the lake, he discovers he is no longer yellow. He's what you get when you mix yellow and blue – green.

Full Story

The Yellow Blob lived in a yellow world where everything was yellow.

Yellow trees.

Yellow grass.

Yellow flowers…

Wherever you looked, it was all yellow.

Yellow house.
Yellow windows.
Yellow door…

When the Yellow Blob painted his hall, he didn't worry about which colour. He chose yellow. Primrose yellow. When he bought carpet for his stairs, the same thing happened. He got yellow. Sunshine yellow. And his bedroom was yellow too.

Yellow bed.
Yellow duvet.
Yellow pillow…

One day the Yellow Blob woke up in the morning and his room was filled with yellow sunshine. He knew it was a day for an adventure. So he jumped out of bed. BLUMP!

He bounced down the stairs. BOUNCETY… BOUNCETY… BOUNCETY…

"I must have something to eat," he said and went into his yellow kitchen. There on the table was just what he fancied. Yes, it was a banana. So he peeled the banana and ate it up. But he still felt hungry. So he looked in the fridge and saw some yellow custard. YUM! It was delicious! And when he'd finished the custard, he went on his way. He went out of the door and down the road. CHICK-A-BOOM… CHICK-A-BOOM…

Soon he came to the yellow moor where all the tussocks of grass were yellow. BOUNCETY… BOUNCETY… BOUNCETY…

Further and further he went, and higher and higher. Until …
BUMPETY BUMP …

The Yellow Blob had met a hill. The Yellow Blob looked up at the hill. It was high - VERY HIGH. "That's not going to put me off," he said. "I'll climb that hill, I will, I will."

So the Yellow Blob started to climb. ERCH… ERCH… ERCH…

PHEW! He felt hot. After stopping for a minute, he started again… ERCH…
ERCH… till he got to the top. "Hooray," said the Yellow Blob, "I did it."

But when the Yellow Blob saw what was on the other side of the hill, he
gasped. WOW!

On the other side of the hill was a big blue lake. The lake looked up. The
Yellow Blob looked down. The water was blue and it looked very inviting.

Then the lake began to sing:

"Come on down, Yellow Blob.
Come down here for a swim.
It's lovely, it's cool.
If you wait, you're a fool.
Come on down, Yellow Blob,
Come on down."

The Yellow Blob said, "I think I will."

So he stretched on his toes… One…. two…. three…. and he jumped. Down
into the cool blue water. SPLASH!

First he swam under the water …SWISH… Then … SWISH… SWISH…
he swam to the side. SWISH… he pulled himself out.

And when he looked at himself,
he had a big surprise.

The Yellow Blob saw he had changed.
He wasn't the Yellow Blob any more.
He was what you get when you mix
yellow and blue.

He was GREEN.

So that's the story of how the Yellow Blob
became the Green Blob. And next time
you think of a story, maybe it'll be the story
of the Green Blob and all the things that he did.

Hints on telling

◉ You can tell the story with some paper and paint to demonstrate what happens when you put blue paint on yellow.

Paint a large spot of yellow to show the Yellow Blob. Then paint a large patch of blue to represent the lake. Then paint a large spot of yellow onto the blue when the Yellow Blob jumps into the lake. Show how that patch of colour goes green.

◉ While you are telling the story, encourage the children to imitate and join in with all the actions – bouncing, eating, climbing, swimming.

Follow-up activities

Give the children a chance to try out the magic of colours themselves with supplies of yellow and blue paint.

Variations

1. Depending on how far you want to take the story, you can try making up other adventures for the Yellow Blob, or the Green Blob.

2. Or you can just discuss some ideas briefly with the children and go on to tell other colour stories. What about The Little Red Monkey on page 22?

Five little monkeys
– a counting rhyme with actions

One of many well-known songs in which five characters or objects are reduced to none, this is excellent as a fun approach to teaching numeracy.

Five little monkeys jumping on the bed

One fell off and bumped his head.

Mummy called the doctor

And the doctor said:

"No more monkeys jumping on the bed."

Four little monkeys jumping on the bed

until:

No little monkeys jumping on the bed!

Hints on telling

- ⊙ Repeated actions and a strong sing-song tone of voice help children follow and learn this rhyme.

- ⊙ Hold up the appropriate number of fingers at the beginning of the rhyme, reducing them appropriately with each verse.

- ⊙ Or have five children come out front to 'be' the monkeys.

- ⊙ Touch your head dramatically to suggest the bump on the head.

- ⊙ Make a phoning gesture when mother calls the doctor.

- ⊙ Wag your finger reprovingly when the doctor speaks.

- ⊙ Sound exaggeratedly sad when you get to the very last line.

The Little Red Monkey

– retold from the picture-book, Little Red Monkey, by John Astrop

Children love this story. The little monkey's theme tune helps them to join in and remember the different episodes.

Story summary

A naughty monkey plays tricks on the creatures of the jungle. They get fed up and decide to teach him a lesson. They trap him in a hole in the jungle and keep him there until he realises why and promises to be better in future.

Full Story

Once in the jungle there lived a little red monkey who was always playing tricks.

One day, he went to see the hippopotamus. The hippopotamus was wallowing in the mud at the time, but when he came out of the mud, the little red monkey painted pink spots on his back. The hippopotamus roared, "Who painted these spots on my back?"

And who was it? The little red monkey.

Another day, the little red monkey went to see the parrot. He saw the parrot's long tail of coloured feathers and pulled it. Yank! The parrot squawked, "Who's pulling my tail?"

And who was it? The little red monkey.

Another day, the little red monkey went to visit the birds' nest. When the birds flew off to find some food, he put sharp prickly thorns in their nest.

"Ouch!" said the birds when they came back. "Who's put these sharp prickly thorns in our nest?"

And who was it? The little red monkey.

The same thing happened with the little animals. He woke them with his drums when they were taking their afternoon sleep. And he tied the elephant's trunk in a knot with the result that the elephant could hardly speak, "Who died my drunk in a dot?"

Finally the animals got so fed up, they decided to teach the little red monkey a lesson. They called a meeting and asked the elephant what they should do. The elephant thought about it (after they'd untied the knot in his trunk) and came up with a plan. "What do little red monkeys like to eat?" he asked.

"Bananas," the animals replied.

The elephant suggested they dig a hole in the jungle and fill it with bananas. When the little red monkey came along, he would start eating the bananas and, without realising what was happening, he would sink down into the hole. Then they would have him trapped in one place for once and they could tell him why they were angry.

That's what the animals did. They dug a hole, filled it with bananas and waited. When the little red monkey came along, he started eating the bananas and by the time he'd finished, he'd sunk down to the bottom of the hole. When he realised where he was, the little red monkey was frightened. "Get me out!" he shouted.

The animals came and looked down the hole. They reminded the little red monkey of all the tricks he had played.

"Do you remember what you painted on my back?" said the hippopotamus. "Do you remember what you did to my tail?" asked the parrot. "Do you remember what you put in our nest?" said the birds. "Do you remember how you woke us up?" said the little animals. "Do you remember what you did to my trunk?" said the elephant.

"But I'll be good from now on," said the little red monkey.

"Please get me out of the hole."

So they did. The elephant put down his trunk and lifted the red monkey out. Then the little red monkey did all kinds of things to make up for the naughty things he had done. Everyone was very happy.

Hints on telling

⊙ Introducing a song – The Little Red Monkey's Song – is an effective way to get and keep attention and to link the episodes of this story:

La la la la

La la la la

What shall I do today I wonder?

Tap your knees in rhythm with the first two lines, rub your hands together gleefully during the third.

⊙ Find some way to bring each of the tricks to life with sound and action. Paint spots on the hippo's back, pull the parrot's tail (Yank!), show the birds flying away from the nest, bang the drums etc.

⊙ Encourage the children to participate in the story by joining in with your actions and sounds.

⊙ When it comes to eating the bananas, pretend to unpeel them and eat them and take your time so that the children can get the idea. Count the bananas. Let the children join in.

⊙ Invite children to contribute and discuss their own ideas. When the animals have their meeting to talk about what to do with the little red monkey, the children can say what they think. Some will probably say, "Kill him!" or "Get the police." Don't shout them down, just discuss the pros and cons of their ideas with them. When the animals have to think about getting the monkey out of the hole, ask the children how this could be done. They will probably come up with lots of different plans.

Follow-up activities

1. This is a particularly good story for encouraging children to make their own pictures. Invite them to choose their favourite moment in the story as the basis of their picture.

2. Talk to children about their pictures. Inscribe what they say onto the bottom of their pictures.

3. Collect the pictures together into a book. Children will love to look at their book again and again.

Storytime Four

The Sea is Deep
– an imagination game

Simple rhymes such as this one enable you to set the scene for a story. They stir children's imaginations and allow them to contribute their ideas. This rhyme is about the sea.

The sea is deep,

The sea is wide.

The sea's got lots of things inside

It's got …? ………….. fishes?

Show an action to represent fishes. Then repeat the rhyme, encouraging everyone to join in.

And I wonder what else the sea has got inside it?

The sea is deep,

The sea is wide.

The sea's got lots of things inside.

It's got fishes and …? ……….a crab?

Ask the person who has suggested a crab for an action to represent it. Or suggest one yourself. Again, encourage everyone to echo the gesture. Then continue:

And I wonder what else is in the sea?

The sea is deep,

The sea is wide.

The sea's got lots of things inside.

It's got fishes and a crab and…? ………. seaweed?

Once more, ask for a gesture, encourage everyone to join in and continue until you feel it's time to stop.

Hints on telling

- Movements of your hands can suggest the depth and width of the sea, also that your audience is being invited to say what the sea may have inside it. Raised eyebrows and an expectant look on your face help them know that it's now their turn to contribute.

- It's vital to come up with an action or gesture for each of the sea's contents as it gets added to the game. This helps everyone to remember the sequence and build it up.

- Children usually volunteer an appropriate action or gesture to go with the idea that has been given. If they don't, you may have to help out.

- Children appreciate it very much if you mirror the particular way they make their gesture.

- It is often helpful to find a sound-effect for an item as well as a gesture.

Variations

1. Try setting the game in a forest instead of the sea:

   The forest is deep and the forest is wide.

   The forest's got lots of things inside.

   It's got…? .... foxes?

   And I wonder what else?

2. Or what about a castle?

   Let's go round the castle. What can we see?

   It's big and old.

   Just follow me!

   Look here!

   What's this? … treasure?

   And I wonder what else we'll see?

26

Fatima the Fish Gets a Fright

– a 'feelings' story

This is one of a series of stories (another appears on page 44) which deals with common emotions, in this case the fear of getting lost and being in danger, then the relief when the fear is over and everything is alright again.

 ## Story summary

Fatima the Fish goes out to meet her new friends. On the way she sees a shark. She gets frightened but manages to get home safely. She tells the story of what happened and her new friends come to find her.

 ## Full Story

This is going to be a frightening story – and it's going to be about a fish. I wonder what the fish could be called? Something beginning with "f"? Fatima?

Fatima the Fish woke up one day, and this is what I heard her say:

I don't know what will happen to me today.

I don't know how I'll feel.

BUT...

......I'm going OUT.

Fatima the Fish was looking forward to seeing her new friends. She'd met them once when she swam to the other side of her usual rocks. Now she was hoping to see them again.

So Fatima the Fish said all her goodbyes. "Goodbye," she said to her mother. "Goodbye!" she said to her father. "See you later."

(You can add other goodbyes to her brothers and sisters).

Then Fatima went swimming out of her cave.

Fatima the Fish swam straight for the rocks. She knew the rocks very well. She knew all the short cuts for getting between them and all the hiding places where you could play peek-a-boo. But today Fatima swam straight past the rocks and on past the seaweed forest. She'd seen the seaweed forest a few times before. She knew it was big and you could easily get lost there. Today she didn't want to get lost. She wanted to find her new friends.

Fatima the Fish went swimming on. "Not far now," she thought. But soon after passing the seaweed forest, Fatima thought she saw a big open mouth. "It's a shark!" she said. "It must be a shark!" And it seemed to be coming straight towards her. "Oh no!" said Fatima the Fish to herself. "I must get out of the way or it might eat me!"

So Fatima the Fish turned round very quickly. Before a second had passed, she was swimming for home as fast as her fins could take her.

Fatima was feeling frightened. She was sure the shark was chasing her. She was sure the shark was right behind her.

Actually, it wasn't! It wasn't coming after her! It hadn't even seen her!

But Fatima didn't know that.

Quickly, Fatima swam past the seaweed forest. Quickly, she swam for the rocks near her home. She thought, "If I can get to the rocks, I'll hide in one of my hiding places. Then I will be safe." So Fatima went on swimming till she got to the rocks. Quickly, she swam into one of the tiniest cracks. There she hid until she dared to peer out.

When Fatima looked out of her hiding place, she couldn't see an open mouth. She couldn't see a shark at all. She peered a little further out. She thought the shark had probably gone. But Fatima knew she must still be careful. So as she swam out from her hiding place, she looked all around her, again and again. But the shark was nowhere to be seen.

So Fatima the Fish went swimming home. When she came to her cave, she felt quite wobbly. But she was very relieved. She'd managed to get home safe. She told her family all about what had happened.

"Clever Fatima," said her mother. "Clever Fatima for swimming so fast. Clever Fatima for hiding in the rocks. None of us like sharks, they're much too big and hungry. So well done, Fatima, for getting out of the way."

Fatima's mother gave her a nice fishy hug. Fatima's father gave her a fishy hug too and so did all her brothers and sisters. Now Fatima felt much, much better.

Then something even nicer happened. Fatima was just about to have a snack when she heard cheerful voices outside her cave. It was her new friends!

"Hello Fatima," said the fishes. "We didn't see you so we've come to find you. Do you want to come out to play?"

Fatima was pleased and excited to see her new friends again. She told them her frightening story - how she'd been coming to look for them when she saw a shark. Her new friends said, "That's funny. We don't usually see sharks in this part of the ocean. Maybe it was a shark who was lost! Perhaps he was trying to find his way home! Anyway, let's go out and play peek-a-boo in the rocks. And your brothers and sisters can come too."

So that's what they did. They had a wonderful time. And, funnily enough, after that frightening day, Fatima the Fish never saw a shark again.

Hints on telling

- ⊙ Capture the feelings of this story in your voice but do not overdo it. You should not want to frighten your audience. You are telling them a story.

- ⊙ Encourage the children to speak about the story by predicting what might happen.

- ⊙ Help the story to remain 'a story' by enabling children to join in with any sounds and gestures you make.

Follow-up activities

1. Drawing different 'feelings' faces onto paper plates makes a good preparation for this sort of story.

2. Making a mobile for the story would be a good follow-up too. The mobile can combine the relevant alphabet letter 'F' with cut-out pictures that illustrate the story.

Magic Pot

– an imagination game

This is a pretending game where everyone pretends to have their own little magic pot. The trick is to encourage children to use their imaginations to find different things inside the pot.

Cup your hands together to suggest the pot. Your upper hand is the lid of the pot. You can move it aside to peer into the pot and see what's hidden inside.

> Here's a little magic pot!
> Look inside and see what you've got!

After telling everyone what you think is inside your pot, suggest that they can do the same. Formalise the game by repeating the rhyme after each child has had a go:

> Here's a little magic pot!
> Look inside and see what you've got!

Allow time for each child to have a turn if they want to.

Variations

Other versions of this game exist with slightly different wordings of the rhyme. This is a simplified version. You can alter it as you wish.

1. Names of children can be added. For example:
   Amy's got a magic pot!
   Look inside, Amy, and see what you've got!

2. Particular themes can be added on different occasions: specifying a theme can help stimulate the children to come up with ideas. For instance, you could suggest that each person finds a different animal in their magic pot. Or you could think of different sorts of food. Or find different places in the pot such as the beach, the forest or a shop. Or you could find different characters from nursery rhymes or picture books.

Magic Cooking Pot

– a traditional English folktale

Magic is the theme of this story! It could lead to lots of discussion about various other kinds of magic – making things vanish, making things bigger – and then that could lead to all kinds of new stories.

 ## Story summary

A little girl is given a magic cooking pot which makes plentiful amounts of porridge for her and her mother. One day when the girl is not at home, the mother asks the pot to make more porridge but doesn't know how to stop it. The porridge overflows until the girl comes home and stops the pot by saying the right words.

Once there was a little girl who lived with her mother. They were very, very poor.

One day there was no food to eat. So the mother sent her daughter out to the forest to collect some berries for their supper.

On the way, the little girl met an old woman. The old woman noticed that the girl looked very hungry.

"Yes," said the little girl, "I am very hungry."

The old woman said she could help. She got out a little cooking pot and gave it to the girl. She told her how to work it. She said that the little girl must always say this little rhyme to make the pot start:

"Hiss and bubble, little cooking pot.
Make some porridge and make it hot."

When the pot had made enough porridge, the little girl must stop it working by saying another little rhyme.

The little girl took the pot home and told her mother all about it. Then she said the rhyme to make it start working.

The little pot started hissing and bubbling and lots of porridge came up inside it. Soon there was plenty of porridge for supper and the little girl told the pot to stop:

"Thank you, little cooking pot.
Now it's time for you to stop."

The porridge was delicious and the little girl and her mother were very happy. For the first time for a long time, they had enough to eat!

Every day after that, the little girl would get out her pot and make food for her and her mother. But one day when the little girl was out playing, the mother got out the pot and told it to make some porridge:

"Hiss and bubble, little cooking pot.
Make some porridge and make it hot."

The pot started hissing and bubbling and lots of porridge came up inside it. When the pot was full, the mother tried to stop it. But she didn't use the right words. What she said was, "That's enough, little cooking pot." And those weren't the right words to use!

So the pot carried on hissing and bubbling and more and more porridge came up inside it. Soon porridge was pouring over the sides of the table. It was flowing out of the kitchen door. It was covering the garden. It was everywhere!

Luckily after a while, the little girl came home. When she saw all the porridge everywhere, she rushed into her house and said the right words to the pot:

> "Thank you, little cooking pot.
> Now it's time for you to stop."

Then the pot stopped making porridge and there was a lot of clearing up to do.

After that, it was only the little girl who used the pot. She always remembered the exact words to use and she and her mother always had just the right amount to eat.

Hints on telling

Preparing the children is half the battle. It will help them get ready for the magic.

- Get out a little cooking pot – a pretend one or a real one – and talk about rhymes that might encourage it to work some magic. You could make up a rhyme together.

- Or you could simply say that you've got a story about a magic pot that made porridge and introduce the rhyme from the story:

  > "Hiss and bubble, little pot
  > Make some porridge, and make it hot!"

- And what about bringing out a box of porridge oats?

Now you are ready to tell the story!

Storytime Six

What to do with a piece of cloth?

– an imagination game

All you need for this game is an interesting colourful piece of cloth. Pieces of cloth can serve many purposes in a storytelling setting. The idea is to encourage children to use their imaginations and show or voice what they come up with.

Tap your knees and click your fingers as you start the first line of the rhyme below. As you say lines two and three, tap your knees and open your hands in an inquiring gesture.

Here's a very fine piece of cloth.
But what's it for? What's it for?

Now ask the children if anyone has an idea of what the cloth could be for. Maybe there's a boy in your group called Abdul who suggests it could be used for a cloak. You can then invite Abdul to come out to the front and show how he would use the cloth as a cloak. You might comment: "That's a good idea, Abdul. Look at Abdul wearing his cloak." Then continue:

So Abdul says it's for a cloak.

But could it be for anything else?

Let's see!

Here's a very fine piece of cloth.

But what's it for?

What's it for?

Maybe someone called Tracey says … "A bedcover!" Again, Tracey can come out to the front and demonstrate her idea. Again, you might comment: "That's a good idea, Tracey. Look at Tracey pulling up her bedcover. Goodnight Tracey!" Then continue:

So Abdul says it's for a cloak.

Tracey says it's for a bedcover.

But could it be for anything else?

Let's see!

And so on!

Allow plenty of time for this activity. Lots of children will want to have a go!

Variations

1. If you've got a piece of cloth that could be a prop in another story, you could bring the game to an end as follows:

   And I've got an idea as well.

   Perhaps the cloth is for telling a story!

   And shall I get ready to tell you the story?

2. The game is adaptable in other ways too. Instead of using a cloth, try a piece of string:

   Here's a nice long piece of string.

   But what could it be for?

   What could it be for?

3. Or what about a woolly hat?

   Here's a nice warm woolly hat

   But where could you go in this hat, do you think?

   Where could you go in this hat?

   To school? To a football match? Out to play?

4. With older children, the game can be varied to encourage more transformative ideas: the cloth could become a magic garden, a peacock's tail, etc.

The Naughty Little Mouse

– a traditional tale

Story summary

A mouse goes out and persuades three shopkeepers into:

1. Giving her some cloth
2. Making her a hat
3. Decorating the hat

Then the mouse manages to persuade the queen into letting her sit on the throne for a day. When she gets home, she's got a good story to tell – and a pretty hat!

Full Story

There was once a little mouse who one day went out for a walk. As she went along she sang her song: "La la, la la, la la, la la."

Soon the mouse came to a shop - a shop that sold cloth. The mouse went into the shop.

"Give me a piece of your cloth," she said to the man inside.

"No," said the man, "You're just a mouse."

"Give me a piece of your cloth," said the mouse, "Or I'll come back here tonight with all of my friends and we'll eat all the cloth in your shop."

"O-o-h!" said the man. "Go away. You're a very naughty little mouse."

Then the mouse remembered a word she could use. "Oh P-L-E-A-S-E?" she said.

"That's better," said the man. "Now you've said 'please', I'll give you a piece of cloth. But only a small piece."

The man went into the back of the shop where he kept his scissors. He cut a small piece of cloth. When he came back, he gave it to the mouse. She was very pleased. She took the cloth and went out of the shop, singing her song as she went down the road: "La la, la la, la la, la la."

Then she came to another shop – a shop that made hats. The mouse went inside.

"Make me a hat from my piece of cloth," she said to the lady inside.

"No," said the lady looking up from her sewing. "You're only a mouse. Get out of my shop."

"Make me a hat from my piece of cloth," said the mouse, "Or I'll come back here with my friends tonight and we'll eat holes in all the hats in your shop."

"T-s-h!" said the lady. "You are a very NAUGHTY little mouse."

"Oh P-L-E-A-S-E?" said the little mouse.

"Very well then," said the lady. "You did say 'please'. So I'll make you a hat. But just a plain one."

The lady took the cloth from the little mouse and sewed it into a hat. When she brought it out, the little mouse was very pleased. She put it on and went out of the shop, singing her song as she went down the road: "La la, la la, la la, la la."

Down the road, the naughty little mouse came to another shop that sold pretty things for decorating clothes – buttons and braids and silk flowers and sequins. The mouse went inside.

"Sew some pretty things onto my hat," she said to the man inside.

"No," said the man. "You're just a mouse. Get out of my shop."

"Sew some pretty things onto my hat," said the little mouse, "Or I'll come back here with my friends tonight and we'll eat up all the stuff in your shop."

"Off with you," said the man. "You're a very naughty little mouse."

"Oh P-L-E-A-S-E?" said the little mouse.

"Very well then," said the man. "You did say 'please'. So I'll sew some pretty things onto your hat. But just a few!"

The man took the hat to the back of the shop and decorated it. When he brought it back, it looked very pretty and the little mouse was very pleased. She put it on and went out of the shop and as she went she sang her song: "La la, la la, la la, la la."

Soon she came to the gates of the palace where the queen lived. The mouse ran inside and looked around till she came to the throne where the queen was sitting. The throne was covered with red velvet cushions.

"Let me sit on your throne," said the mouse.

"No," laughed the queen. "You're only a mouse."

"If you don't let me sit on your throne," said the mouse, "I'll come back here with all my friends tonight, and we'll eat your red velvet cushions."

"Dear me," said the queen. "You're a very naughty little mouse".

"Oh P-L-E-A-S-E!" said the naughty little mouse.

"Very well then," said the queen. "You did say 'please'. You can sit on my throne. But only for one day!"

The queen got up and went out of the room. The naughty little mouse ran up the side of the throne and sat on the red velvet cushions. She felt so proud as she looked around. But at the end of the day, she remembered her house and wanted to go home. She ran down the throne, out of the palace and along the road and as she went, she sang her song: "La la, la la, la la, la la."

When the mouse got home, she was so tired she went straight to bed. But she didn't take her hat off. She slept in it all night long and in the morning when she woke, she went out of the house to go and find her friends. And when she found them, she told them everything that had happened the day before. She told them exactly the story I've just told you now.

Hints on telling

◉ Props can make this story come to life. Find a little wooden or tin box that can contain some things you can use in the course of the story. Put in the box a small toy mouse (the kind you get in a pet shop is fine) and also a selection of the things that the hatmaker might use for sewing (needles, thread etc). Then prepare two similar little hats; one plain, one decorated with sequins or braid. Put these, too, inside your sewing box together with one or two small pieces of the material from which you have made the hats.
The items can be brought out at appropriate times – mouse first, then a piece of material, next the plain hat and finally the decorated hat.

◉ The mouse's song can be as simple as you like. Hold your toy mouse in front of you moving her along through the air as you sing the song. Encourage everyone to join in the singing.

◉ Use different tones in your voice to good effect. Use your voice to convey the dialogue between the different characters. The mouse varies between being very demanding and rather whining. The other characters vary between crossness and being a bit more sympathetic.

Follow-up activities

1. Invite the children to draw pictures of the story.

2. Let the children make maps of the mouse's journey. Draw onto some sheets of paper simple winding roads onto which the children can add pictures of the shops and the palace.

3. Do craftwork based on the story. Set up tables with materials for making mouse figures (e.g. corks for the body, card for the ears and nose, coloured wool for tails etc). Also set out materials for making hats for the mouse – pieces of cloth, glue and sequins or braid.

The Fly Called "Eee"

– a participative story adapted from a traditional Tamil tale from Sri Lanka

This story provides a good chance to practise your animal noises and learn some new ones from your audience. When I first heard it, it was told in a very simple style. You can follow that example, putting the story into your own words, or you can make the story highly participative, inviting individual children to come out and 'perform' for the others.

 ## Story summary

One day, the fly forgets his name –" Eee". He goes to look for some creatures who may be able to remind him what he is called. But the creatures he comes across speak only their own languages. At last he finds someone who can help him. In the traditional Sri Lankan version, this creature was a horse – the neigh of the horse sounds like "eee" – but in my version, it's a child who helps by remembering the name.

Simple Story

In the faraway country of Sri Lanka, the fly has got a special name: "Eee" (to rhyme with bee).

But one day, something awful happened. The fly called "Eee" forgot his name. (What a thing to do! You wouldn't do that, would you?) This is how it came about.

When "Eee" woke up in the morning, he tried to remember his name but however hard he tried, he couldn't do it. He felt so upset and worried that he decided to go out of his house and look for someone who might help him.

None of the creatures he met could help him. They only said their own sounds.

Then at last he met some children. (You can pretend the fly has come into your own nursery or school if you like.) He asked them his name and they all said: "Eee!"

Hints on telling

- After the fly has met the dog and cat, ask the children if they can think of any other animals that could be in the story and if they can make their noises.

- When hands go up, invite a child to come out to the front to be in the story. Pick up the idea by pretending to be the fly asking the 'animal' if he or she knows your name: "Can you possibly tell me my name?" After the child has made the animal noise, you could sound a bit sad that it's not your name but then, as the storyteller, cheerfully thank the child for taking part in the story and give the child a clap. Even very shy children often take the chance to participate in this story. Many rise to the occasion with enormous humour.

- Or you can tell the story in my rap version on the next page.

Rap Version - By Mary Medlicott

Once upon a time
There was a fly called "Eee".
Who's He?
"That's me!" said the fly called "Eee".

Well one sunny day, that fly he went to bed
And he woke up in the morning
With a pain in his head.
So he went to the doctor
And the doctor said, "Name?"
"Please will you tell me your name?"

The fly said, "SURE!
Course I'll tell you my name.
My name is ... Oh! I've forgotten my name!
I've gone and forgotten my name!
Now nothing will ever be the same...
Unless there's someone who can tell me my name."

So the fly got up and flew down the road
Looking for a friend.

Down the road he met the dog.
"Scuse me, Dog," said the fly.
"Can you possibly tell me my name?"
The Dog said "WOOF! WOOF! WOOF! WOOF!"
(He could only speak dog language.)

But the fly said "No, that's not MY name.
That's definitely not my name.
Now nothing will ever be the same
if I can't remember my name."

So the fly got up and flew on down the road,

Looking for a friend.

Down the road he met the Cat...

"Scuse me, Cat," said the Fly. "Can you please tell me my name?"

The Cat replied, "MEEAOW..."

(Repeat as above as the fly meets lots of different animals according to the children's suggestions. The children join in making appropriate sounds and if you wish, they can come out to the front to be the particular animal.)

(Finally, of course, the fly must meet someone who can tell him his name. Could it be a child? The children in your group? Whoever it is, make sure the fly sounds very, very pleased when you and the children tell him that his name is "Eee".)

"Yes! Yes!" said the Fly

"That is my name. That definitely is my name.

Now everything can be the same

Because you've remembered my name.

Thank you."

And that is the end of my game.

Hints on telling

⊙ Tap your knees and click your fingers in rhythm with the words of the rhyme: tap... click... tap... click... tap... click... tap... Don't worry if you're no good at clicking. Many of your audience won't be able to do it either, tapping your knees will do instead. But it's important to make the action feel cheerful and fun - joining in with the rhythm helps children focus and participate.

Andy the Ant Gets Angry

Another 'feelings' story by Mary Medlicott
– this one deals with anger.

Story summary

Andy the Ant and his family have made a new garden. Andy gets very angry when an elephant blunders towards it because it looks as if the elephant will destroy it. Andy tries to get him to go away and is extremely happy when he succeeds.

Full Story

This is going to be an ANGRY story. It's going to be about an ant – an ant called Andy.

Andy the Ant woke up one day and this is what I heard him say:
"I don't know what will happen to me today
I don't know how I'll feel,
BUT...
I'm going OUT!"

It was early in the morning. Andy the Ant was very excited. He wanted to walk round his new garden. Andy's family was enormous – brothers, sisters, aunties, uncles, cousins, grandparents, mothers, fathers. They all lived together in the same little house and, in the last few weeks, Andy had been helping make a special new garden to give them a bit more space to relax in. Only yesterday, Andy had helped finish the garden with a fine new garden gate.

"Today," Andy thought, "the first thing I'll do is walk round the new garden to see if I like it."

He went straight outside. But what was that? What was that terrible noise? Something ... somebody... was coming along...
along the path towards Andy's new garden.

It was …

something … somebody … with very big feet

something … somebody … with very big legs

something … somebody…with a very big body

something … somebody …. with a very big head

something … somebody…with very big ears

something… somebody … with a very big trunk

It was an ELEPHANT!

Boom … went the elephant's feet.

Boom…. boom….

The elephant was getting closer. Soon he would be stepping on Andy's new garden.

Suddenly Andy felt angry. He didn't feel frightened. He just felt angry. All that work, that lovely new garden. The elephant would smash it. He would ruin it all.

Without delay, Andy peered through the gate and shouted,

"Go away, Elephant! Go back! Go away!"

But Elephant didn't hear. He just kept coming closer.

Boom … went the elephant's feet.

Boom … Boom …

Andy shouted again. "Go away, Elephant, can't you hear me? You're not looking where you're going. Go away."

But Elephant didn't take any notice. He just kept coming closer.

Boom... went his elephant's feet.

Boom... boom...

By now Andy was very angry. Very, very angry indeed. Once again he shouted, and this time he did it so loudly he thought he was going to pop.

"STOP, ELEPHANT! LOOK WHERE YOU'RE GOING. GO AWAY!"

Suddenly Elephant stopped. "What's that squeaking?" he said in a deep rumbling voice that almost deafened Andy. "Who's there? What do you want?"

"It's ME," Andy answered. "Andy the Ant. I'm down here by the garden gate. You're coming too close to our garden. You're going to step on it. Please go away."

"Oh sorry," Elephant replied, looking down at Andy. "I didn't mean to upset you. I didn't plan on hurting your garden. I didn't even know you'd been making a garden. I'll go the other way."

And before you could say Hip Hip Hooray, Elephant turned in his tracks and went lumbering off in another direction.

"Phew!" said Andy. "That was a close one." And he went back into the house. He wasn't a bit angry any more. He just felt glad, and very relieved.

Inside the house, Andy's mother was getting things ready for breakfast.

Andy told her what had happened.

"Well done Andy," said his mother. "Sometimes it's worth getting angry."

Then she gave him a hug and a nice cup of tea and Andy felt happy, and very, very proud.

Hints on telling

- It's important to communicate the emotion in your face and voice but never in a way that is itself frightening.

- Use a big deep rhythmical voice to suggest the elephant's footsteps.

- Look up when you're taking the part of Andy, down when you're talking in the voice of the elephant.

- Make the ending sound very reassuring and happy.

 ## Making up other similar stories

- You can follow a basic pattern if you want to make up new stories along similar lines. First choose a feeling. Then choose a creature who will experience the feeling. Next choose a name for the creature. An alphabetical match between the feeling, the creature and the name is a good idea: it gives rhythm to the story. Thus the angry story has an ant called Andy while the frightening story on page 27 has a fish called Fatima. A happy story could have a hippo called Humphrey.

- The structure of the stories follows a pattern too. First the character in the story goes out. Then something happens which results in the character experiencing the emotion or feeling concerned. There are usually one or two obstacles to overcome. Then the story always ends on a happy note with the character coming back home to hugs and kisses and nice things to eat.

Going on a Bear Hunt
– a traditional action-chant

Since being put into picture book format, this popular, well-known storyteller's chant has achieved huge popularity.

Story summary

In this story, we go out to find a bear and on the way overcome various obstacles. When we finally see the bear, we run away because we think the bear is chasing us. We get home just in time!

Full story

We're going on a bear hunt, a bear hunt, a bear hunt...

Oh what a lovely day!

I'm not scared, I'm not scared...

Oh look ... tall thick grass!

We can't go over it, we can't go under it.

We'll have to make a path through it.

Get ready to make a path through the grass!

SWISH! SWISH! SWISH!

Everybody through?

We're going on a bear hunt, a bear hunt, a bear hunt...

Oh what a lovely day!

I'm not scared, I'm not scared...

Oh look ... squelchy brown mud!

We can't go over it, we can't go under it.

We'll have to go through it.

Get your boots on!

SHLUCK! SHLUCK! SHLUCK!

Everybody through?

We're going on a bear hunt, a bear hunt, a bear hunt...

Oh what a lovely day!

I'm not scared, I'm not scared ...

Oh look ... a fast rushing river!

We can't go over it, we can't go under it.

We'll have to go through it.

Get ready to swim!

SPLASH! SPLASH! SPLASH!

Everybody through?

We're going on a bear hunt, a bear hunt, a bear hunt...

Oh what a lovely day!

I'm not scared, I'm not scared...

Oh look... a deep, dark cave!

We can't go over it, we can't go under it.

We'll have to go inside it.

Get ready to tiptoe inside!

SHH! SHH! SHH!

Everybody see him?

Two big brown eyes, two big furry ears, a big wet nose...

It's a bear! Run!

Back through the river... the mud... the grass...

Back home. Open the door. Up the stairs. Into bed. Hide...

Here's Mum!

"Mum! Guess where I've been!

I've been on a bear hunt and seen a bear. And I wasn't a bit scared."

Were YOU?

Hints on telling

- Before starting, it's a good idea to explain that you are NOT going on a bear hunt to kill a bear or hurt a bear. You are going to SEE a bear.

- Be purposeful and definite. Get your voice into a sing-song mood. Tap your knees in rhythm: We're Going on a BEAR-hunt, a BEAR-hunt, a BEAR-hunt.

- As you spot an obstacle – grasses, mud, river – fix your eyes on an imaginary spot somewhere in front of you and get some drama into your voice: 'OH NO!'

- Use your body. Swing your arms to shove the grasses aside. Lift your legs to pull them through the mud. Swim vigorously through the river.

- When you get to the cave, change your voice to a quiet, hushed voice. If you wish, add new details such as "Ugh! Cobwebs!" as you enter the cave.

- When you see the bear, make spectacle eyes. Put your hands to your head to show his ears. Tap your nose as you refer to his nose.

- Imitate running as you start running away. From this point on, all actions occur in quick motion.

- During the dialogue with mum, pretend to be talking as a child.

Variations

1. Create fresh obstacles such as a frozen lake as the children become familiar with the pattern of the story.

2. Turn the last part of the story into a role-play, for example using cloths over an easel to make a cave where the bear can hide. Take different groups of children to visit the bear. Give children turns at being the bear, practising growling and raising their claws.

3. Turn the whole thing into an action play, physically leading children on the bear hunt. First arrange the classroom, hall or an outside space into appropriate areas. Then all take part in the journey, moving around in a long line.

Rabbit's Lucky Escape

– a folk tale from East Africa

Opportunities for role-play abound in this excellent story which emphasises the value of brains over mere size and strength.

 ## Story summary

Rabbit goes by mistake into Lion's den. When Lion comes back, she has to think quickly to get herself out of trouble. She pretends to be King of the Lions taking a rest in the den. When Lion fetches other friends – Elephant, Snake etc – Rabbit pretends to be King of the Elephants, King of the Snakes etc. Finally when the animals get too suspicious and threaten to come into the den, she says she is King of All the Animals and they must close their eyes and bow down when she comes out because she is too important for them to see her. Thus Rabbit makes her escape.

 ## Full Story

One day Rabbit goes into Lion's den by mistake. She falls asleep. But when Lion comes home, he stops at the entrance. He knows there's someone inside.

"Who's in my den?" he roars. "Come out, or I, Lion, am coming in."

Rabbit wakes up. She is frightened. But she gets a good idea. She pretends to be King of the Lions.

"I'm the King of the Lions," she says in her loudest voice. "I'm having a rest in your den. You'll have to wait."

Lion is not sure what to do. He goes and fetches Elephant. Elephant trumpets, "Who's in my friend Lion's den? Come out or I, Elephant, am coming in."

Rabbit is frightened again. But now she pretends to be the King of the Elephants.

"I'm the King of the Elephants. I'm having a rest in Lion's den. You'll have to wait."

Lion and Elephant are not convinced.
Who is really in Lion's den? Is someone just
pretending to be a King? They go and fetch
Snake. Snake hisses loudly,
"Who's in my friend Lion's den?
Come out or I, Snake, am coming in."

Rabbit pretends to be King of the Snakes.
But the animals can't believe that
so many Kings are inside Lion's den.
They say, "Come out of Lion's den
or we're all coming in."

Now Rabbit is really, really frightened –
until she gets the best idea of all. She
pretends to be King of ALL the Animals.

"Don't you understand?" she shouts in her
loudest, grandest voice. "I'm King of ALL the Animals. And now I've had my
rest, I'm ready to come out of this den. But first you must bow down and
close your eyes for I'm too important for you to see me."

The animals bow down and close their eyes and Rabbit hops out of the den.
Only Lion peeks out of the corner of his eyes. And when he sees who it is,
he goes chasing after her. But by then, Rabbit has reached home and is safe
inside.

Hints on telling

- To set the scene for this story, take a bit of time introducing the two main characters. For Rabbit, make long ears, twitch your nose and show her hoppity, skippety way of moving. For Lion, suggest how hungry he is by rubbing your hands over your stomach and show him walking about with a loping, greedy sort of gait.

  Also introduce the places where the two main characters live. Rabbit has a small little house. Lion has a big shadowy den. Draw them in the air.

- Take the many opportunities for children to join in with what the characters say. Use a big loud voice when Lion and his friends are talking. Use a small high frightened voice when Rabbit is talking to herself about what she is going to do. Use a big confident voice when Rabbit is talking to the animals.

- Show the emotions of the story. Playact being very angry when Lion and his friends get cross: wave your fists in the air or hammer your fists on your knees. Playact being very frightened when Rabbit hears Lion and his friends outside the den: tap your hand against your chest to give the impression of extreme nervousness.

- Invite ideas from the children. Ask the children to suggest which animals Lion went to fetch. Summon up the character of these animals with various gestures or noises. For example, swing an arm in front of your head to suggest Elephant's trunk. Raise your hands to your ears to indicate his large flappy ears. Use your arm and hissing sounds to suggest Snake.

Follow-up activities

1. Invite the children to draw pictures of the story. A series of pictures on a foldout or zig-zag book is effective.

2. Encourage role-play. In your building-blocks area, suggest the children create Rabbit's house and Lion's den. Or whisper the idea that the climbing frame in your outside play area might become Lion's den.

Where are the bees?

– a traditional finger rhyme

This traditional rhyme can be used to help children with counting.

Here is the beehive

But where are the bees?

Far inside where nobody sees.

Open the hive

And out they come

One, two, three, four, five

Hints on telling

- Make your hand into a fist to represent the beehive.

- Point into your fist when you ask where the bees are.

- Unfold your fingers one by one to suggest the bees flying out.

Variations

The last line of the rhyme is sometimes as follows:

bzz...bzz...bzz...bzz...bzz

Two Birds in a Beard

– an adaptation of a folk-story from Thailand

This magical story explains how birds first came to live in trees. It is highly expressive, giving the storyteller lots of opportunities for actions and sounds to help the children join in and, afterwards, to enact and role-play the story.

 ## Story summary

Two birds live in an old man's beard. One day, after the birds' five eggs have hatched, the father bird goes out searching for worms to feed the young ones and becomes trapped overnight inside a flower. When he returns next day, he is met by a very cross female bird and a noisy argument begins. Then the voice of the old man tells the birds that they'll have to go and live somewhere else.

 ## Full Story

Far, far away there was a cave. Behind the cave was a dark, dark forest. Behind the forest were high, high mountains. Behind the mountains was a blue, blue lake. And on the lake grew big white flowers.

In the cave lived an old man who had a long, long, beard. And in the old man's beard there was a nest. And in the nest there lived two birds – Mr Bird and Mrs Bird.

One summer, Mr Bird and Mrs Bird had five eggs in the nest. They took it in turns to sit on the eggs until, one day, the eggs began to hatch.

Soon there were five little birds, all of them calling for food.

"Breakfast, breakfast, breakfast, breakfast, breakfast!"

"Lunch, lunch, lunch, lunch, lunch!"

"Tea, tea, tea, tea, tea!"

"Supper, supper, supper, supper, supper!"

Father Bird and Mother Bird had a busy time trying to keep their chicks well fed. From morning to night, they took it in turns to go out hunting for insects and worms.

But one day, when Father Bird was out searching for food, he had nothing but bad luck. Wherever he looked, he could find no food.

He flew up from the cave into the tall dark trees.

Nothing.

He flew up over the trees to the high, high mountains.

Nothing.

He flew over the mountains to the big, blue lake.

Nothing.

By the time he came to the lovely white flowers, he was extremely tired.

Father Bird flew down to the flowers and came to rest in the centre of the biggest, whitest bloom. And there, at once, he fell fast asleep.

Unfortunately, while he was sleeping, the sun began going down in the sky. And as it went down, the big white flowers began to close their petals. Soon, the biggest flower was tightly shut with Father Bird inside.

When Father Bird woke up from his nap, he couldn't get out of the flower. He couldn't fly upwards without bumping his head. He couldn't fully open his wings. He realised he was trapped. But however loudly he called for help, there was no one to hear him and no one to come to the rescue.

Meantime, back in the nest, Mother Bird was waiting for Father Bird to return. Sometimes she felt anxious about him. Sometimes she felt cross and all round her, the little birds were cheeping.

This went on all night until at last the sun came up in the sky.

And of course, as the sun began to rise over the big blue lake, the lovely white flowers began to open. First, Father Bird saw a crack of light. Then as the crack got bigger and bigger, he discovered he could open his wings. Joyfully, he flew up into the sky and headed home for the nest.

When Father Bird arrived, Mother Bird was waiting for him. "WHERE HAVE YOU BEEN?" she asked.

Father Bird replied. "I've been so worried about you. All night long, I was trapped in a flower."

"Trapped in a flower?" said Mother Bird crossly. "Do you expect me to believe that?"

And, with that, the two birds began to argue. As they argued, their voices got louder and louder. And the little chicks got hungrier and hungrier and began making more and more noise.

Suddenly, they all heard a strange new sound. It was a big, deep voice and it said:

"YOU TWO BIRDS ARE MAKING TOO MUCH NOISE. YOU'LL HAVE TO GO AND LIVE SOMEWHERE ELSE!"

Do you know who it was? It was the old man.

And that's when Father Bird and Mother Bird started looking for another place to make a nest. Luckily, by the time they had found a place they liked, the little birds were learning to fly.

And where do you think they made their new home? On a branch in one of the tall, dark trees.

That's how birds started living in trees. They've been making their nests there ever since.

Hints on telling

⊙ Set the scene by using gestures to conjure up the big cave, the trees, the mountains, the flowers and the old man's long beard. Cross your hands at the wrist and move them gently to suggest the birds flying around. A sense of drama enters the story when the birds' eggs begin to hatch. Cup your hands into an egg shape, then move them quickly to suggest the eggs hatching. Do the same thing five times and your listeners will start joining in. For the flowers, have your hands cupped together. Show your fingers opening out as the flowers open, coming together as they close.

⊙ Emphasise the repetitiveness of the little birds calling for food. This is also a place where children can join in.

Playact Father Bird's distress when he finds he is trapped.

Also playact Mother Bird's different feelings when Father Bird doesn't come home. But be careful to judge how much emotion to use according to the children in your group. For some children, this could be a worrying scene. It is best to keep things light-hearted and as humorous as you can. It's a big surprise in the story when the old man speaks out at the end. Use a deep low voice. The children will probably guess who is speaking.

⊙ Invite children to contribute their ideas to the story. Ask children at the end where the birds might choose to go and live. You could discuss the advantages of different places before saying that actually they went to live in the trees.

Follow-up activities

1. This is a good story for children to act out. You can allocate parts – an old man, Father Bird and Mother Bird, five little children to be the eggs that hatch into chicks.

2. The old man's beard can be a wonderful prop to make – perhaps using long curls of white paper.

Source Notes

Notes on the sources of the action-chants and stories

Mrs Wiggle and Mrs Waggle

This is one of many versions of an action-story that has been kept alive by storytellers working in the oral tradition. Every storyteller's version differs slightly or a lot from every other storyteller's version. The story is often told with male characters, Mr Wiggle and Mr Waggle.

Sun-Frog and Moon-Frog

This story was originally developed by the late Penny Bernand for a Pop-Up Theatre production. Based on the West African folktale of how the sun and moon got into the sky, it has been further embellished by myself in the course of many retellings and has proved immensely popular with young children.

The Yellow Blob

This story popped into my head, whole and complete, one day while I was walking in the park. It has proved popular with children right across the Primary age range.

The Little Red Monkey

This story is closely based on the picture-book by John Astrop, Little Red Monkey (Hutchinson, 1977). Retold here in my own words, the story became one of the first that I consciously 'told' to children. This happened one day when I made up a theme song for the little red monkey and realized that I knew the picture book so well, I could bring the story to life without the book.

Fatima the Fish Gets a Fright

This story is one of a long series of stories which I started making up when a nursery school asked me for some stories about 'feelings'. I discovered that this kind of story worked particularly well with ethnically mixed groups of children. In choosing names from those the children knew, it was possible to introduce a wide variety of names that do not generally appear in the published stories that are usually available to nurseries and early years classes.

Magic Cooking Pot

This well-known folktale has been retold in many printed versions. There are many similar tales of magic kettles and so on in countries across the world.

The Naughty Little Mouse

This story, too, was passed on to me at a workshop. Told at the workshop by an Indian woman, it is one I have retold many times, always with great thanks to the person who passed it on to me and with pleasure in the children's response.

The Fly Called "Eee"

This highly participative story is an adaptation of a folktale which was told to me by a refugee mother from Sri Lanka who came to a storytelling course I was running. I gratefully acknowledge her original story which I have adjusted in various ways over many times of telling, including making the story into a rap.

Andy the Ant Gets Angry

This story was actually the first of my 'feelings' stories. I discovered that the stories worked especially well if I consulted the children on what feeling they would like to have a story about, then let them choose a name for the main character. With my help, they chose names which shared the same first letter with the selected feeling. I also encouraged the children to do a lot of guessing and predicting about what was going to happen next.

Going on a Bear Hunt

Michael Rosen's version of this traditional rhyme is available as a Big Book (Walker Books, 1997). Many variants of the rhyme can be found in America and elsewhere.

Rabbit's Lucky Escape

Another debt of gratitude is owed to the person who told me this story at a storytelling workshop some time ago. Her background was Asian, though she grew up in East Africa, and she said she had often heard it told in her family when she was growing up.

Two Birds in a Beard

This story was told me in a workshop by a woman from Thailand who recalled it as being part of a longer story which she had heard as a child. It seems to me to provide a very complete experience as it is.

Resources List

Some books about storytelling, story collections and other storytelling resources

Books about storytelling

Teresa Grainger, **Traditional Storytelling in the Primary Classroom;** Scholastic
A practical guide to storytelling with primary age children and related classroom activities.

Elizabeth Grugeon and Paul Gardner, **The Art of Storytelling for Teachers and Pupils;** David Fulton
A handbook on storytelling and how it relates to current literacy initiatives.

Vivian Gussin Paley, **The Boy who would be a Helicopter: Storytelling in the Classroom;** Harvard University Press
An American teacher's account of working with a kindergarten class where stories are placed at the heart of the curriculum.

Some collections of stories

Hugh Lupton, **The Story Tree: Tales to Read Loud;** Barefoot Books
A collection of stories with the emphasis on oral storytelling

Mary Medlicott, **The Little Book of Storytelling;** A&C Black
A collection of stories and other material for telling to young children.

Sophie Windham, **The Orchard Book of Nursery Stories;** Orchard Books
Simple straightforward tellings of well-known traditional tales for young children.